THE
QUOTABLE
JESUS

Honor Books

Tulsa, Oklahoma

The Quotable Jesus
ISBN 1-56292-822-8
Copyright © 2000 by Honor Books
P.O. Box 55388
Tulsa, Oklahoma 74155
Printed in Mexico.

Manuscript prepared by Todd Hafer, Kansas City, Kansas

Introduction

The lowly carpenter's son from Nazareth lived and died almost two thousand years ago. His life, which lasted only thirty-three years, was not remarkable on any grand scale. In fact, He lived in relative obscurity until three years before His death. When He did move out of the shadows and speak openly, the words of this unpretentious folk leader were recorded by only a few of His twelve disciples.

Nevertheless, the simple words of Jesus Christ have endured throughout the centuries, inspiring, motivating, and enriching the lives of millions of people. Today, most of the world's population is familiar with His teachings, and His devotees reside in every nation on earth.

For this reason, we have selected a variety of Jesus' words as recorded in the New Testament. We then categorized our selections so you, the reader, can apply His extraordinary wisdom to your own life and see what Jesus Christ had to say about His earthly mission and His relationship with God.

We hope as you read this book, you will sense the power that resides in the words of Jesus Christ—power to change long-standing perceptions, power to rethink priorities, power to live a truly significant and fulfilled life.

JESUS
TEACHES
ABOUT
GOD . . .

With God all things are possible.

—MATTHEW 19:26 KJV

*God so loved the world that he gave his one
and only Son, that whoever believes in him
shall not perish but have eternal life.*

—JOHN 3:16

*If you then, who are evil, know
how to give good gifts to your children,
how much more will the heavenly Father
give the Holy Spirit to those who ask him?*

—LUKE 11:13 RSV

*God is a Spirit: and they that worship him
must worship him in spirit and in truth.*

—JOHN 4:24 KJV

*Do not be afraid, little flock, for your Father
has been pleased to give you the kingdom.*

—LUKE 12:32

*Your Father knows exactly what
you need even before you ask him!*

—MATTHEW 6:8 NLT

Will not God bring about justice
for his chosen ones, who cry out to him
day and night? . . . I tell you, he will
see that they get justice, and quickly.

—LUKE 18:7-8

For he is not a God of the dead, but
of the living: for all live unto him.

—LUKE 20:38 KJV

---

*God did not send his Son into
the world to condemn the world,
but to save the world through him.*

—JOHN 3:17

*My Father's will is that everyone
who looks to the Son and believes
in him shall have eternal life.*

—JOHN 6:40

What God has joined together,

let man not separate.

—MARK 10:9

Do not test the Lord your God.

—LUKE 4:12 NLT

*The Father loves the Son
and shows him all he does.*

—JOHN 5:20

*My Father is always at his work to
this very day, and I, too, am working.*

—JOHN 5:17

JESUS
REVEALS
HIMSELF ...

The Father and I are one.

—JOHN 10:30 NLT

I tell you the truth, the Son can do nothing by himself; he can do only what he sees his Father doing, because whatever the Father does the Son also does.

—JOHN 5:19

I am the way and the truth and
the life. No one comes to the
Father except through me.

—JOHN 14:6

I am the bread of life; he who comes
to me shall not hunger, and he who
believes in me shall never thirst.

—JOHN 6:35 RSV

I am the light of the world. Whoever follows me will never walk in darkness, but will have the light of life.

—JOHN 8:12

I am the root and the offspring of David, the bright morning star.

—REVELATION 22:16 RSV

I am the Alpha and the Omega.

—REVELATION 22:13

I am the first and the last.

—REVELATION 1:17 RSV

I am the Living One; I was dead,
and behold I am alive for ever and ever!

—REVELATION 1:18

I am the good shepherd; I know
my sheep and my sheep know me.

—JOHN 10:14

Take my yoke upon you and learn from me,

for I am gentle and humble in heart,

and you will find rest for your souls.

—MATTHEW 11:29

My yoke is easy, and my burden is light.

—MATTHEW 11:30 RSV

*Here I am! I stand at the door
and knock. If anyone hears my voice
and opens the door, I will come in.*

—REVELATION 3:20

*Follow me, and I will
make you fishers of men.*

—MATTHEW 4:19 RSV

*Anyone who does not carry his cross
and follow me cannot be my disciple.*

—LUKE 14:27

My kingdom is not of this world.

—JOHN 18:36

In this world you will have trouble.
But take heart! I have overcome the world.

—JOHN 16:33

I give them eternal life, and
they shall never perish; no one
can snatch them out of my hand.

—JOHN 10:28

I tell you the truth, if anyone keeps

my word, he will never see death.

—JOHN 8:51

This is the will of him who sent me,

that I shall lose none of all that he has

given me, but raise them up at the last day.

—JOHN 6:39

Because I live, you will live also.

—JOHN 14:19 RSV

Surely I am with you always,
to the very end of the age.

—MATTHEW 28:20

JESUS TEACHES ABOUT THE KINGDOM OF GOD . . .

I must preach the Good News of the Kingdom of God . . . that is why I was sent.

—LUKE 4:43 NLT

I tell you the truth, no one can see the kingdom of God unless he is born again.

—JOHN 3:3

The kingdom of God does not come with your careful observation, nor will people say, "Here it is," or "There it is," because the kingdom of God is within you.

—LUKE 17:20-21

What is the Kingdom of God like? How can I illustrate it? It is like a tiny mustard seed planted in a garden; it grows and becomes a tree, and the birds come and find shelter among its branches.

—LUKE 13:18-19 NLT

Let the little children come to me . . . for the kingdom of God belongs to such as these.

—MARK 10:14

I tell you the truth, anyone who will not receive the kingdom of God like a little child will never enter it.

—MARK 10:15

*Again I tell you, it is easier for a camel
to go through the eye of a needle than for
a rich man to enter the kingdom of God.*

—MATTHEW 19:24 RSV

*I tell you the truth, the tax collectors
and the prostitutes are entering the kingdom
of God ahead of you. For John came to you
to show you the way of righteousness,
and you did not believe him, but the
tax collectors and the prostitutes did.*

—MATTHEW 21:31-32

The kingdom of God is near.
Repent and believe the good news!

—MARK 1:15

No one who puts his hand to the plow
and looks back is fit for the kingdom of God.

—LUKE 9:62 RSV

No one who has left home or wife or
brothers or parents or children for
the sake of the kingdom of God will fail
to receive many times as much in this age
and, in the age to come, eternal life.

—LUKE 18:29-30

I tell you, among those born of women
there is no one greater than John;
yet the one who is least in the
kingdom of God is greater than he.

—LUKE 7:28

*Do not set your heart on what you will
eat or drink; do not worry about it.
For the pagan world runs after all such
things, and your Father knows that you
need them. But seek his kingdom, and
these things will be given to you as well.*

—LUKE 12:29-31

You are not far from the kingdom of God.

—MARK 12:34 RSV

JESUS
REVEALS
HIS MISSION . . .

He who sent me is reliable, and what
I have heard from him I tell the world.

—JOHN 8:26

I must preach the good news of the
kingdom of God . . . that is why I was sent.

—LUKE 4:43

The stone rejected by the builders

has now become the cornerstone.

—MATTHEW 21:42 NLT

Upon this rock I will build my church,

and all the powers of hell will not conquer it.

—MATTHEW 16:18 NLT

I am the light of the world. Whoever follows me will never walk in darkness, but will have the light of life.

—JOHN 8:12

I am the good shepherd. The good shepherd lays down his life for the sheep.

—JOHN 10:11

I am the resurrection and the life.
Those who believe in me, even though
they die like everyone else, will live again.

—JOHN 11:25 NLT

I have come as a light to shine in this dark
world, so that all who put their trust in me
will no longer remain in the darkness.

—JOHN 12:46 NLT

You will know the truth, and
the truth will set you free.

—JOHN 8:32

I came to bring truth to the world.
All who love the truth recognize
that what I say is true.

—JOHN 18:37 NLT

The Son of Man did not come to
be served, but to serve, and to give
his life as a ransom for many.

—MATTHEW 20:28

Healthy people don't need a doctor—
sick people do. . . . I have come to
call sinners, not those who think
they are already good enough.

—MATTHEW 9:12-13 NLT

If a man owns a hundred sheep, and one of them wanders away, will he not leave the ninety-nine on the hills and go to look for the one that wandered off?

—MATTHEW 18:12

The Son of Man came to seek and to save what was lost.

—LUKE 19:10

The Spirit of the Lord is on me,
because he has anointed me to preach
good news to the poor. He has sent me to
proclaim freedom for the prisoners.

—LUKE 4:18

This is what is written: The Christ
will suffer and rise from the dead on the
third day, and repentance and forgiveness
of sins will be preached in his name.

—LUKE 24:46-47

The Son of Man must suffer many
things . . . he must be killed and
on the third day be raised to life.

—LUKE 9:22

The Son of Man . . . will be handed over
to the Gentiles. They will mock him, insult
him, spit on him, flog him and kill him.
On the third day he will rise again.

—LUKE 18:31-33

As Moses lifted up the serpent in the
wilderness, so must the Son of man
be lifted up, that whoever believes
in him may have eternal life.

—JOHN 3:14-15 RSV

Now my heart is troubled, and what shall
I say? "Father, save me from this hour"?
No, it was for this very reason
I came to this hour.

—JOHN 12:27

I, the Son of Man, feast and drink, and you say, "He's a glutton and a drunkard, and a friend of the worst sort of sinners!" But wisdom is shown to be right by the lives of those who follow it.

—LUKE 7:34-35 NLT

Do not think that I have come to abolish the Law or the Prophets; I have not come to abolish them but to fulfill them.

—MATTHEW 5:17

Don't imagine that I came to bring peace to the earth! No, I came to bring a sword.

—MATTHEW 10:34 NLT

There is a terrible baptism ahead of me, and I am under a heavy burden until it is accomplished.

—LUKE 12:50 NLT

*The Son of Man did not come to
be served, but to serve, and to give
his life as a ransom for many.*

—MARK 10:45

*This is my blood of the covenant,
which is poured out for many.*

—MARK 14:24 RSV

I am the way, and the truth, and the life;
no one comes to the Father, but by me.

—JOHN 14:6 RSV

Just as the Father raises the dead and
gives them life, even so the Son gives
life to whom he is pleased to give it.

—JOHN 5:21

I have come in my Father's name.

—JOHN 5:43

My food is to do the will of him who sent me, and to accomplish his work.

—JOHN 4:34 RSV

Jesus
Prays
to God
His Father . . .

I pray not for the world, but for them which
thou hast given me; for they are thine.

—JOHN 17:9 KJV

Neither pray I for these alone,
but for them also which shall
believe on me through their word.

—JOHN 17:20 KJV

Forgive us our debts, as we
also have forgiven our debtors.

—MATTHEW 6:12

Father, forgive them, for they
do not know what they are doing.

—LUKE 23:34

My Father, if it is not possible
for this cup to be taken away unless
I drink it, may your will be done.

—MATTHEW 26:42

My God, my God,
why have you forsaken me?

—MARK 15:34 NLT

Father, into your hands

I commit my spirit.

—LUKE 23:46

It is finished!

—JOHN 19:30 NLT

This is the way to have eternal life—
to know you, the only true God, and
Jesus Christ, the one you sent to earth.

—JOHN 17:3 NLT

I praise you, Father, Lord of heaven
and earth, because you have hidden these
things from the wise and learned, and
revealed them to little children.

—LUKE 10:21

JESUS
CALLS
HIS
DISCIPLES...

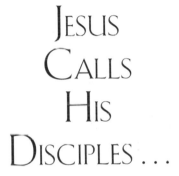

Come, be my disciple.

—LUKE 9:59 NLT

If anyone would come after me,
he must deny himself and take
up his cross and follow me.

—MATTHEW 16:24

If anyone is ashamed of me and my words,
the Son of Man will be ashamed of him
when he comes in his glory and in the glory
of the Father and of the holy angels.

—LUKE 9:26

Every one who acknowledges me
before men, I also will acknowledge
before my Father who is in heaven.

—MATTHEW 10:32 RSV

If you hold to my teaching, you are really my disciples. Then you will know the truth, and the truth will set you free.

—JOHN 8:31-32

No one can become my disciple without giving up everything for me.

—LUKE 14:33 NLT

He who does not gather with me, scatters.

—LUKE 11:23

Not everyone who says to me, "'Lord, Lord,"
will enter the kingdom of heaven,
but only he who does the will of
my Father who is in heaven.

—MATTHEW 7:21

I am the one who corrects and disciplines everyone I love. Be diligent and turn from your indifference.

—REVELATION 3:19 NLT

To him who overcomes and does my will to the end, I will give authority over the nations.

—REVELATION 2:26

*If the world hates you, keep in
mind that it hated me first.*

—JOHN 15:18

*Be faithful, even to the point of death,
and I will give you the crown of life.*

—REVELATION 2:10

Anyone who does the will of
my Father in heaven is my
brother and sister and mother!

—MATTHEW 12:50 NLT

If you love me, you will
obey what I command.

—JOHN 14:15

JESUS
CAUTIONS
HIS FOLLOWERS . . .

*Watch out! Be on your guard against
all kinds of greed; a man's life does not
consist in the abundance of his possessions.*

—LUKE 12:15

It is more blessed to give than to receive.

—ACTS 20:35 KJV

Listen and understand. What goes into a man's mouth does not make him "unclean," but what comes out of his mouth, that is what makes him "unclean."

—MATTHEW 15:10-11

A good person produces good deeds from a good heart, and an evil person produces evil deeds from an evil heart. Whatever is in your heart determines what you say.

—LUKE 6:45 NLT

Beware of the teachers of the law. They like to walk around in flowing robes and love to be greeted in the marketplaces and have the most important seats in the synagogues.

—LUKE 20:46

These people honor me with their lips, but their hearts are far from me. They worship me in vain.

—MATTHEW 15:8-9

When you are brought before synagogues, rulers and authorities, do not worry about how you will defend yourselves or what you will say, for the Holy Spirit will teach you at that time what you should say.

—LUKE 12:11-12

I will give you the right words and such wisdom that none of your opponents will be able to reply!

—LUKE 21:15 NLT

Do not be afraid; keep on speaking,
do not be silent. For I am with you.

—ACTS 18:9-10

I tell you this, that you must
give an account on judgment day
of every idle word you speak.

—MATTHEW 12:36 NLT

Do not swear by your head, for you cannot make even one hair white or black. Simply let your "Yes" be "Yes," and your "No," "No."

—MATTHEW 5:36-37

Do not swear at all: either by heaven, for it is God's throne; or by the earth, for it is his footstool.

—MATTHEW 5:34-35

This is the verdict: Light has come into the world, but men loved darkness instead of light because their deeds were evil.

—JOHN 3:19

Whoever lives by the truth comes into the light, so that it may be seen plainly that what he has done has been done through God.

—JOHN 3:21

*There is nothing concealed that will
not be disclosed, or hidden that will not
be made known. What you have said
in the dark will be heard in the daylight.*

—LUKE 12:2-3

*No good tree bears bad fruit, nor again
does a bad tree bear good fruit; for
each tree is known by its own fruit.*

—LUKE 6:43-44 RSV

Whoever wants to become great
among you must be your servant, and
whoever wants to be first must be your slave.

—MATTHEW 20:26-27

He who is least among you all—
he is the greatest.

—LUKE 9:48

JESUS
INSTRUCTS
HIS FOLLOWERS . . .

You know the commandments:
"Do not commit adultery, do not murder,
do not steal, do not give false testimony,
honor your father and mother."

—LUKE 18:20

Do for others what you would like them to
do for you. This is a summary of all that
is taught in the law and the prophets.

—MATTHEW 7:12 NLT

Love your enemies. Do good to those who hate you. Pray for the happiness of those who curse you. Pray for those who hurt you.

—LUKE 6:27-28 NLT

Love your enemies and pray for those who persecute you, so that you may be sons of your Father who is in heaven.

—MATTHEW 5:44-45 RSV

I tell you the truth, this poor widow has put more into the treasury than all the others. They all gave out of their wealth; but she, out of her poverty, put in everything—all she had to live on.

—MARK 12:43-44

Give, and it will be given to you; good measure, pressed down, shaken together, running over, will be put into your lap.

—LUKE 6:38 RSV

*Be careful not to do your "acts of
righteousness" before men, to be seen
by them. If you do, you will have
no reward from your Father in heaven.*

—MATTHEW 6:1

*Sell everything you have and give to the poor,
and you will have treasure in heaven.*

—LUKE 18:22

Do not work for food that spoils,
but for food that endures to eternal life.

—JOHN 6:27

It is written, "Man shall
not live by bread alone."

—LUKE 4:4 RSV

Let your light shine before men,
that they may see your good deeds
and praise your Father in heaven.

—MATTHEW 5:16

"Well done, good and faithful servant!
You have been faithful with a few things;
I will put you in charge of many things."

—MATTHEW 25:23

Let the children come to me.
Don't stop them! For the Kingdom
of God belongs to such as these.

—LUKE 18:16 NLT

See that you do not look down on
one of these little ones. For I tell you
that their angels in heaven always see
the face of my Father in heaven.

—MATTHEW 18:10

*Love one another. As I have loved you,
so you must love one another. By this
all men will know that you are my
disciples, if you love one another.*

—JOHN 13:34-35

*"Love the Lord your God with
all your heart and with all
your soul and with all your mind."
This is the first and greatest commandment.*

—MATTHEW 22:37-38

You shall love your neighbor as yourself.

—MARK 12:31 RSV

If someone strikes you on one cheek,
turn to him the other also.

—LUKE 6:29

*Give to Caesar what is Caesar's
and to God what is God's.*

—MARK 12:17

Freely you have received, freely give.

—MATTHEW 10:8

Do not store up for yourselves treasures
on earth, where moth and rust destroy,
and where thieves break in and steal.

—MATTHEW 6:19

Sell what you have and give to those in need.
This will store up treasure for you in heaven!
And the purses of heaven have no holes
in them. Your treasure will be safe.

—LUKE 12:33 NLT

Your eye is a lamp for your body.
A pure eye lets sunshine into your soul.

—LUKE 11:34 NLT

If you are filled with light, with no dark
corners, then your whole life will be radiant,
as though a floodlight is shining on you.

—LUKE 11:36 NLT

Worship the Lord your God
and serve him only.

—LUKE 4:8

Be perfect, therefore, as
your heavenly Father is perfect.

—MATTHEW 5:48

JESUS COMFORTS HIS DISCIPLES . . .

Come to me, all you who are weary and burdened, and I will give you rest.

—MATTHEW 11:28

Can all your worries add a single moment to your life? Of course not. . . . So don't worry about tomorrow, for tomorrow will bring its own worries. Today's trouble is enough for today.

—MATTHEW 6:27, 34 NLT

Don't worry about everyday life—
whether you have enough food, drink,
and clothes. Doesn't life consist of
more than food and clothing?

—MATTHEW 6:25 NLT

Look at the birds. They don't need to plant or
harvest or put food in barns because your
heavenly Father feeds them. And you are
far more valuable to him than they are.

—MATTHEW 6:26 NLT

Look at the lilies and how they grow.
They don't work or make their clothing,
yet Solomon in all his glory was not
dressed as beautifully as they are.

—LUKE 12:27 NLT

If God cares so wonderfully for flowers
that are here today and gone tomorrow,
won't he more surely care for you?

—LUKE 12:28 NLT

Look at my hands and my feet. It is I myself!
Touch me and see; a ghost does not have
flesh and bones, as you see I have.

—LUKE 24:39

Peace I leave with you; my peace
I give you. . . . Do not let your hearts
be troubled and do not be afraid.

—JOHN 14:27

If you only knew the gift God has for you and who I am, you would ask me, and I would give you living water.

—JOHN 4:10 NLT

The water I give them takes away thirst altogether. It becomes a perpetual spring within them, giving them eternal life.

—JOHN 4:14 NLT

The wind blows wherever it pleases.
You hear its sound, but you cannot tell
where it comes from or where it is going.
So it is with everyone born of the Spirit.

—JOHN 3:8

It is not for you to know the times
or dates the Father has set by his own
authority. But you will receive power
when the Holy Spirit comes.

—ACTS 1:7-8

Where two or three come together

in my name, there am I with them.

—MATTHEW 18:20

Do not let your hearts be troubled.

Trust in God.

—JOHN 14:1

You will grieve, but your
grief will turn to joy.

—JOHN 16:20

You have sorrow now, but I will see you
again and your hearts will rejoice, and
no one will take your joy from you.

—JOHN 16:22 RSV

No, I will not abandon you as

orphans—I will come to you.

—JOHN 14:18 NLT

Surely I am with you always,

to the very end of the age.

—MATTHEW 28:20

JESUS
BLESSES
THE PEOPLE ...

Blessed are the pure in heart,

for they will see God.

—MATTHEW 5:8

Blessed are the meek, for

they will inherit the earth.

—MATTHEW 5:5

Blessed are those who mourn,

for they will be comforted.

—MATTHEW 5:4

Blessed are those who hunger and thirst

for righteousness, for they will be filled.

—MATTHEW 5:6

Blessed is the man who does
not fall away on account of me.

—LUKE 7:23

Even more blessed are all who hear
the word of God and put it into practice.

—LUKE 11:28 NLT

Blessed are you when people insult you, persecute you and falsely say all kinds of evil against you because of me. Rejoice and be glad, because great is your reward in heaven.

—MATTHEW 5:11

Blessed are you who weep now, for you will laugh.

—LUKE 6:21

Blessed are the peacemakers,
for they will be called sons of God.

—MATTHEW 5:9

Blessed are those who are persecuted
because of righteousness, for theirs
is the kingdom of heaven.

—MATTHEW 5:10

JESUS COMMISSIONS HIS FOLLOWERS ...

The harvest is so great,

but the workers are so few.

—LUKE 10:2 NLT

Go into all the world and preach

the good news to all creation.

—MARK 16:15

You will be my witnesses in
Jerusalem, and in all Judea and Samaria,
and to the ends of the earth.

—ACTS 1:8

He who hears you hears me, and he
who rejects you rejects me, and he who
rejects me rejects him who sent me.

—LUKE 10:16 RSV

*I am sending you . . . to open their eyes
and turn them from darkness to light,
and from the power of Satan to God.*

—ACTS 26:17-18

*Go therefore and make disciples of all nations,
baptizing them in the name of the Father
and of the Son and of the Holy Spirit.*

—MATTHEW 28:19 RSV

As long as it is day, we must
do the work of him who sent me.

—JOHN 9:4

As the Father has sent me,
I am sending you.

—JOHN 20:21

*Be dressed ready for service and
keep your lamps burning, like men
waiting for their master to return.*

—LUKE 12:35-36

*It will be good for those servants whose
master finds them ready, even if he comes
in the second or third watch of the night.*

—LUKE 12:38

The seed on good soil stands for those with a noble and good heart, who hear the word, retain it, and by persevering produce a crop.

—LUKE 8:15

There is joy in the presence of God's angels when even one sinner repents.

—LUKE 15:10 NLT

*Do not rejoice that the spirits submit
to you, but rejoice that your names
are written in heaven.*

—LUKE 10:20

*When you enter a house, first say,
"Peace to this house." If a man of peace
is there, your peace will rest on him;
if not, it will return to you.*

—LUKE 10:5-6

*When you enter a town and are
welcomed, eat what is set before you.
Heal the sick who are there and tell them,
"The kingdom of God is near you."*

—LUKE 10:8-9

*But when you enter a town and are not
welcomed, go into its streets and say,
"Even the dust of your town that sticks to
our feet we wipe off against you. Yet be sure
of this: The kingdom of God is near."*

—LUKE 10:10-11

I tell you the truth, anyone who gives

you a cup of water in my name

because you belong to Christ

will certainly not lose his reward.

—MARK 9:41

Feed my lambs.

—JOHN 21:15 RSV

Jesus
Teaches
about
Love,
Faith, and
Forgiveness ...

*The reason my Father loves me is
that I lay down my life—only to take it
up again. No one takes it from me, but
I lay it down of my own accord.*

—JOHN 10:17-18

*God so loved the world that he gave his one
and only Son, that whoever believes in him
shall not perish but have eternal life.*

—JOHN 3:16

*As the Father has loved me, so have
I loved you. Now remain in my love.*

—JOHN 15:9

*Greater love has no one than this,
that he lay down his life for his friends.*

—JOHN 15:13

Love your enemies! Pray for those who persecute you! In that way, you will be acting as true children of your Father in heaven.

—MATTHEW 5:44-45 NLT

If you love only those who love you, what good is that? Even corrupt tax collectors do that much. If you are kind only to your friends, how are you different from anyone else?

—MATTHEW 5:46-47 NLT

I tell you the truth, if you have faith as small as a mustard seed, you can say to this mountain, "Move from here to there" and it will move. Nothing will be impossible for you.

—MATTHEW 17:20-21

I tell you the truth, anyone who has faith in me will do what I have been doing. He will do even greater things than these.

—JOHN 14:12

Everything is possible for him who believes.

—MARK 9:23

Listen to me! You can pray for anything,
and if you believe, you will have it.

—MARK 11:24 NLT

*Because you have seen me, you
have believed; blessed are those who
have not seen and yet have believed.*

—JOHN 20:29

According to your faith will it be done to you.

—MATTHEW 9:29

*When you stand praying, if you hold
anything against anyone, forgive him,
so that your Father in heaven
may forgive you your sins.*

—MARK 11:25

*If you forgive men when they sin against you,
your heavenly Father will also forgive you.*

—MATTHEW 6:14

If your brother sins, rebuke him,
and if he repents, forgive him.

—LUKE 17:3

If he [your brother] sins against you seven
times in a day, and seven times comes back
to you and says, "I repent," forgive him.

—LUKE 17:4

He who has been forgiven little loves little.

—LUKE 7:47

Friend, your sins are forgiven.

—LUKE 5:20

JESUS
TEACHES
ABOUT
PRAYER ...

*My house shall be called a
house of prayer for all nations.*

—MARK 11:17 RSV

*When you pray, say: "Father, hallowed
be your name, your kingdom come. Give us
each day our daily bread. Forgive us our sins,
for we also forgive everyone who sins against
us. And lead us not into temptation."*

—LUKE 11:2-4

*When you pray, go away by yourself,
shut the door behind you, and pray to
your Father secretly. Then your Father,
who knows all secrets, will reward you.*

—MATTHEW 6:6 NLT

*When you pray, do not keep on babbling
like pagans, for they think they will be
heard because of their many words.*

—MATTHEW 6:7

Love your enemies and pray for those who persecute you, that you may be sons of your Father in heaven.

—MATTHEW 5:44-45

When you are praying, first forgive anyone you are holding a grudge against, so that your Father in heaven will forgive your sins, too.

—MARK 11:25 NLT

Ask and it will be given to you;
seek and you will find; knock and
the door will be opened to you.

—MATTHEW 7:7

If you remain in me and my words
remain in you, ask whatever
you wish, and it will be given you.

—JOHN 15:7

Be always on the watch, and pray.

—LUKE 21:36

Pray that you will not be

overcome by temptation.

—LUKE 22:40 NLT

Jesus Teaches about Things to Come . . .

Behold, I am coming soon! My reward is with me, and I will give to everyone according to what he has done.

—REVELATION 22:12

Behold, I am coming soon! Blessed is he who keeps the words of the prophecy in this book.

—REVELATION 22:7

*To him who overcomes, I will give
the right to eat from the tree of life,
which is in the paradise of God.*

—REVELATION 2:7

*Therefore keep watch, because you do not
know on what day your Lord will come.*

—MATTHEW 24:42

From now on, the Son of Man will be
seated at the right hand of the mighty God.

—LUKE 22:69

The Son of Man in his day will be like
the lightning, which flashes and lights
up the sky from one end to the other.

—LUKE 17:24

When the Son of man comes,

will he find faith on earth?

—LUKE 18:8 RSV

Those who are considered worthy of taking

part . . . in the resurrection . . . can no

longer die; for they are like the angels.

—LUKE 20:35-36

Heaven and earth will pass away,

but my words will not pass away.

—MARK 13:31 RSV

I tell you the truth, whoever

hears my word and believes him

who sent me has eternal life.

—JOHN 5:24

Because I live, you will live also.

—JOHN 14:19 RSV

*I tell you the truth, a time is coming
and has now come when the dead
will hear the voice of the Son of God
and those who hear will live.*

—JOHN 5:25

*A time is coming and has now come
when the true worshipers will worship
the Father in spirit and truth.*

—JOHN 4:23

*They are God's children, since they
are children of the resurrection.*

—LUKE 20:36

JESUS CHALLENGES THE PEOPLE ...

This is what is written: The Christ will suffer and rise from the dead on the third day, and repentance and forgiveness of sins will be preached in his name.

—LUKE 24:46-47

Everything written about me by Moses and the prophets and in the Psalms must all come true.

—LUKE 24:44 NLT

*When you have lifted up the Son
of Man, then you will know that
I am the one I claim to be.*

—JOHN 8:28

*When I am lifted up on the cross,
I will draw everyone to myself.*

—JOHN 12:32 NLT

*Whoever eats my flesh and drinks
my blood remains in me, and I in him.*

—JOHN 6:56

*Whoever blasphemes against the
Holy Spirit will never be forgiven;
he is guilty of an eternal sin.*

—MARK 3:29

From everyone who has been given much, much will be demanded; and from the one who has been entrusted with much, much more will be asked.

—LUKE 12:48

Whoever has will be given more; whoever does not have, even what he thinks he has will be taken from him.

—LUKE 8:18

*A prophet is honored everywhere
except in his own hometown and among
his relatives and his own family.*

—MARK 6:4 NLT

*Whoever does the will of my Father in
heaven is my brother and sister and mother.*

—MATTHEW 12:50

*Whoever can be trusted with very
little can also be trusted with much.*

—LUKE 16:10

*Whoever is dishonest with very
little will also be dishonest with much.*

—LUKE 16:10

Because of the increase of wickedness,

the love of most will grow cold, but he

who stands firm to the end will be saved.

—MATTHEW 24:12-13

There will always be temptations to sin,

but how terrible it will be for

the person who does the tempting.

—LUKE 17:1 NLT

If anyone causes one of these little ones who believe in me to sin, it would be better for him to be thrown into the sea with a large millstone tied around his neck.

—MARK 9:42

You experts in the law, woe to you, because you load people down with burdens they can hardly carry, and you yourselves will not lift one finger to help them.

—LUKE 11:46

Why don't you judge for yourselves
what is right? As you are going with
your adversary to the magistrate, try
hard to be reconciled to him on the way.

—LUKE 12:57-58

Be merciful, just as your Father is merciful.

—LUKE 6:36

Do not give dogs what is sacred;

do not throw your pearls to pigs.

—MATTHEW 7:6

I am sending you out as lambs among wolves.

—LUKE 10:3 NLT

I ask you, which is lawful on the
Sabbath: to do good or to do evil,
to save life or to destroy it?

—LUKE 6:9

The Sabbath was made for man,
not man for the Sabbath. So the
Son of Man is Lord even of the Sabbath.

—MARK 2:27-28

O unbelieving generation . . .
How long shall I put up with you?

—MARK 9:19

"My temple will be a place of prayer," but
you have turned it into a den of thieves.

—LUKE 19:46 NLT

Anyone who looks at a woman lustfully has already committed adultery with her in his heart.

—MATTHEW 5:28

You are the ones who justify yourselves in the eyes of men, but God knows your hearts.

—LUKE 16:15

If your hand or foot causes you
to sin, cut it off and throw it away.

—MATTHEW 18:8 NLT

The spirit is willing, but the body is weak.

—MATTHEW 26:41

No one can serve two masters. Either he will hate the one and love the other, or he will be devoted to the one and despise the other. You cannot serve both God and Money.

—MATTHEW 6:24

What good will it be for a man if he gains the whole world, yet forfeits his soul? Or what can a man give in exchange for his soul?

—MATTHEW 16:26

*He who does not honor the Son does
not honor the Father, who sent him.*

—JOHN 5:23

He who hates me hates my Father also.

—JOHN 15:23 RSV

*I tell you, my friends, do not be
afraid of those who kill the body
and after that can do no more.*

—LUKE 12:4

By standing firm you will gain life.

—LUKE 21:19

Why do you look at the speck of sawdust in
your brother's eye and pay no attention
to the plank in your own eye?

—LUKE 6:41

If any one of you is without sin,
let him be the first to throw a stone.

—JOHN 8:7

Do not judge, or you too will be judged.
For in the same way you judge
others, you will be judged.

—MATTHEW 7:1-2

With the measure you use, it will
be measured to you—and even more.

—MARK 4:24

THE
CHALLENGE ...

Whoever believes in him is not condemned,
but whoever does not believe stands
condemned already because he has not believed
in the name of God's one and only Son.

—JOHN 3:18

Anyone who listens to my teaching
and obeys me is wise, like a person
who builds a house on solid rock.

—MATTHEW 7:24 NLT

Repent, for the kingdom of heaven is near.

—MATTHEW 4:17

Additional copies of this book
are available from your local bookstore.

If you have enjoyed this book,
or if it has impacted your life,
we would like to hear from you.

Please contact us at:

Honor Books
Department E
P.O. Box 55388
Tulsa, Oklahoma 74155
Or by e-mail at info@honorbooks.com